The ABC's of Hershey
The Reading Therapy Dog

Written by Dr. Donna J. Snyder

**The ABC's of Hershey:
The Reading Therapy Dog**

Copyright © 2023 Dr. Donna J. Snyder

ISBN:
978-1-963177-55-8
978-1-963177-74-9

All rights reserved. No parts of this publication can be reproduced or transmitted in any form or by any means, electronically or mechanically including photocopying, recording, or any information or retriveval system, without prior written permission of the author, Dr. Donna J. Snyder.

The ABC's of Hershey: The Reading Therapy dog

Table of Contents

Dedication	1
Let's Meet Hershey	2
The ABC's of Hershey: The Reading Therapy Dog	8
Reflection Pages with PAL Hershey	36
Extend the Fun with PAL Hershey (Child-friendly Ideas)	45
Extend the Fun with PAL Hershey (Parents, Guardians, Volunteers, Para-educators)	49
Goals and Objectives of The ABC's of Hershey: The Reading Therapy Dog	57
Benefits of Reading Therapy Dogs	66
Glossary	68
Acknowledgements	71
Meet the Team	74
Stay Connected with PAL Hershey	77
Additional Sources	78
Thank You from PAL Hershey	81

Dedication

This book is dedicated to the PAL Teams and all Therapy Animal Reading Teams whose passion is to bring serenity, love, and joy to others. And, to all readers, young and old, who enjoy the comfort, support and affirmation that reading therapy dogs provide. May these relationships continue to grow and flourish! This book is also dedicated to PAL Hershey, whose unconditional love, patience, and kindness fill my days with tremendous joy.

Lastly, this book is dedicated to Greg K., a lifelong friend who gave Hershey to us as a gift when Hershey was 1 year old. Without Greg's generosity and unconditional love, Hershey would not have become our well-loved family member and therapy dog.

Let's Meet Hershey!

I'm so happy that you are going to read a story about me and how I love to go to school! Before we begin, I want you to get to know a little about me.

I'm five-pound Yorkie (smallest of the Terrier breed of dogs). I have lots of things that make me special and unique, just like you have so many traits and characteristics that make YOU special and unique! I hope that you'll like seeing my pictures and reading the captions so you can get to know me and become one of my very good "furends."

Let's Meet Hershey!

My official AKC name is Gregory's Hershey Kiss. (My name also reminds people of yummy Hershey's chocolate!)

I love superheros! Who is your favorite superhero?

I sure do LOVE going to baseball games! Go NATS!
Do you have a favorite sport or team?

Let's Meet Hershey!

I can be very silly!
What do you do to be silly?

I think it's fun to wear costumes!
What is your most favorite costume to wear?

I do LOVE books!
What are your favorite books?

Let's Meet Hershey!

I love going to school to learn!
What are your favorite subjects at school?

I love birthday parties!
Have you ever been to a birthday party?
What kinds of games did you play?

Sometimes, I zoom around outside in my sportscar!
What do you like to do outside?

Let's Meet Hershey!

I help with home projects. How do you help around your home?

I sleep with my favorite stuffed toys. Do you have a special stuffed animal that you sleep with each evening?

I am a registered therapy dog who visits schools, libraries, nursing homes, senior centers, homeless shelters, and federal government offices. Please join me as I share a day in my life as a reading therapy dog.

People Animals Love (PAL)

As a registered therapy dog, I always wear my PAL bandana and have my PAL notebook with me.

Here we go....Our day begins!

The ABC's of Hershey

The Reading Therapy Dog

"A" is for ACTIVE

"A" is for Active listening to all my PAL directions.

"B" is for BEING

"B" is for Being prepared for our visit with a good night's sleep and healthy food selections.

"C" is for COMBING

"C" is for Combing my hair, brushing my teeth and washing my face.

"D" is for DISPLAYING

"D" is for Displaying my PAL therapy dog bandana, in just the right place.

"E" is for EXERCISING

"E" is for Exercising before our PAL visit each day.

"F" is for FROLICKING

"F" is for Frolicking, running and a few minutes of morning play.

"G" is for GATHERING

"G" is for Gathering and organizing our supplies for the school.

"H" is for HELPING

"H" is for Helping and remembering each and every school rule.

 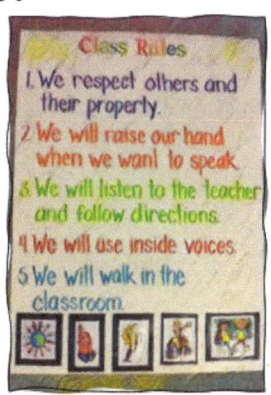

"I" is for IMAGINING

"I" is for Imagining the fun that
I'll soon be able to share.

"J" is for JOY

"J" is for Joy for all of the readers
who show that they care!

"K" is for KNOWING

"K" is for Knowing my therapy job at the school.

"L" is for LEARNING

"L" is for Learning to listen
to readers, an important rule.

"M" is for MASTERING

"M" is for Mastering the 3 "Canine Good Citizen" tests that I took.

"N" is for NOTING

"N" is for Noting and reviewing the rules from the PAL therapy dog handbook.

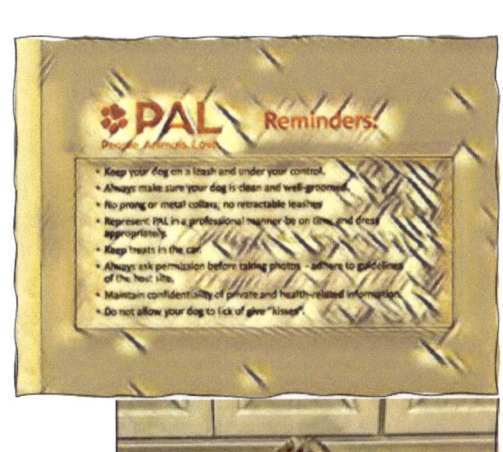

"O" is for OBSERVING

"O" is for Observing a reader's book selection.

"P" is for POSITIONING

"P" is for Positioning myself to secure the best reader and dog connection!

"Q" is for QUALIFIED

"Q" is for Qualified as an AKC therapy dog partner and friend.

"R" is for READY

"R" is for Ready to patiently listen until each book's end!

"S" is for SMILING

"S" is for Smiling when we sit side-by-side.

"T" is for TREASURING

"T" is for Treasuring joy that friends and reading provide.

"U" is for UNDERSTANDING

"U" is for Understanding, supporting and caring.

"V" is for VALUING

"V" is for Valuing what each
reader is carefully sharing.

"W" is for WATCHING

"W" is for Watching and listening as readers turn pages.

"X" is for E**X**CITEMENT

"X" is for eXcitement for readers, of all ages!

"Y" is for YEARNING

"Y" is for Yearning for lots more fun times with you.

"Z" is for ZEALOUS

"Z" is for Zealous for the therapy pet job that I do!

"Pawsitively" Fun Ideas!

Extend the fun of learning with some of PAL Hershey's suggestions.

The following pages are sure to be "dog-gone" fun as you become a "fur-ever" friend with PAL Hershey.

Reflection Pages with PAL Hershey

You can use the following pages to capture your reflections, thoughts, ideas and pictures to send to PAL Hershey.

REFLECTION PAGES

Have some "dog-gone" fun!

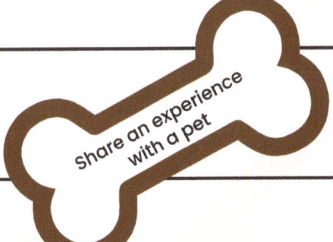

Write to PAL Hershey

Share your thoughts about his book, a favorite section, or something you learned. Or, be creative and write him a story.

Dear PAL Hershey,

Your "furever" friend,

Email your letter to: HersheyAKCtherapydog@gmail.com

Draw a Picture for PAL Hershey

**Draw a picture of you reading to PAL Hershey.
Or, be creative and design your own pictures for PAL Hershey.
He LOVES to see your "adog-able" ideas!**

You can design your "pawsome" ideas here.

Email your drawing to: HersheyAKCtherapydog@gmail.com

Play Words with PAL Hershey

**Playing with words is such a fun way to learn!
PAL Hershey has lots of rhymes in his story. See if you can find them and add your own new rhyming words below.**

Play Words with PAL Hershey

**PAL Hershey LOVES to make you laugh.
He also thinks making silly tongue twisters about him is "paw-fect".
Try creating some tongue twisters about PAL Hershey below.**

Learn New Words with PAL Hershey

**Think about the vocabulary words in PAL Hershey's book.
Jot down "un-fur-miliar" new words below.
Add to the list as you read more books.**

Join PAL Hershey and Help Your Community

**PAL Hershey loves to help his community.
He hopes that you will also love to help your school and community.**

Please share some of your "paw-some" ideas below.

_____

_____

_____

_____

_____

_____

_____

Join PAL Hershey in Spreading Kindness

PAL Hershey is patient, supportive and always kind to his "furends". He wants everyone to feel included and supported.

Think of the many ways you are kind and help others.

_____

_____

_____

_____

_____

_____

_____

New Ideas for PAL Hershey

After reading and rereading the book, what are some ideas that you have for PAL Hershey? What are you wondering about?

PAL Hershey would LOVE to know!

Extend the Fun with PAL Hershey (Child-friendly Ideas)

Want to Write to PAL Hershey?
Feel Like Creating Some Artwork for PAL Hershey?

Here are a Few Ideas for You to Consider:

I would love to receive a note or letter from you. I have listed a few ideas, but I am "paw-sitively" open to your ideas. Not sure what to write about? I have some "pawsome" ideas below, but I just hope that you'll send me a letter or message.

- I love all kinds of books. Please share the books that you want to read with me. Don't forget to tell me why you chose these books.

- Share experiences that you have enjoyed with a dog or a pet.

- I love to help others as a volunteer. Share ways that you like to help at school, home or in your community.

- Share some new learnings, or "ah-ha" moments after reading <u>The ABC's of Hershey: The Reading Therapy Dog.</u>

- I practiced a very long time to pass my three AKC Canine Good Citizen tests. I practiced learning my commands and directions for many months! Each day I focused on improving and getting a little bit better. I worked hard to be able to earn my AKC certificates. I am proud of my efforts. Share some things that you are proud of being able to do.

- What do you think about my routine to get ready for school visits? Are there other things you think I should do to be an even better reading therapy dog?

- What other kinds of books would you like me to write? Why? I love to hear ideas and new possibilities!

- Write a story about a new adventure that you and I could take together.

- I always try to be encouraging and supportive and want each reader to feel comfortable. What are some ways that you help friends feel included, comfortable, and supported?

• Draw and illustrate your favorite part of the book you are currently reading. Don't forget to tell me about your book.

• Draw a picture of you reading to me. Is there a favorite spot or location where the two of us could share a good story together?

• Draw a picture of me at your school. Who will I visit? What grade level? What will the classroom look like?

• I was very proud to earn my awards and was happy to sit beside them and have my picture taken. Draw a picture of one of your proud moments.

• Draw a picture of how you gather and organize your supplies for school. Are any of your school supplies similar to mine?

• I know that daily exercise is important. Draw a picture of how you and I could play together and get some exercise.

• For letter "I" in my book, I like to use my imagination to think about the fun times that I will be able to share with readers. Use your imagination and draw a picture of the fun times that you would like to have if I visited and read with you.

• Be creative and choose one or two alphabet letters and create some new action words for me. Allow your illustrations to bring those letters to life, just like I did in my book.

• Choose your own ideas to write, draw, illustrate or create a message or story for me.

Extend the Fun with PAL Hershey
(Parents, Guardians, Volunteers, Para-educators)

PAL Hershey has some "adog-able" ideas to support your child's literacy development.

I. **Incorporate Questions Before, During, and After Reading <u>The ABC's of Hershey: The Reading Therapy Dog</u>**

Asking children questions during the reading process help them to clarify and comprehend what they are reading. Modeling how to ask questions while reading can help children learn how to build interest in reading and become stronger, more independent readers.

Before Reading (Asking questions before reading help to set a purpose for the story and to activate children's prior learning.)

• Share the front and back covers of the book. What characters do you think will be in this book? Why? (Predicting)

• What do you think a reading therapy dog does? (Predicting)

• What kind of experiences have you had with a dog? How do you think that they will be similar or different from the dog's experiences in this book? (Connecting)

• What are you wondering about as you look at the book's front and back covers? (Questioning)

During Reading (Asking questions during reading help children make connections, monitor their understanding, and help them stay focused on the content.)

• How do you think PAL Hershey feels when he enters the school? Why? (Inferring)

• How is your morning routine similar to or different from PAL Hershey's routine before he goes to school? (Connecting)

• If you were reading to PAL Hershey, how would you feel? (Connecting)

• Is there anything you were wondering about while reading the book? (Questioning)

After Reading (Asking questions after reading a story help children to summarize and reflect on the story and main idea.)

• Tell me the story in your own words. (Summarizing)

• What was the "big idea" in this book? (Inferring)

• Retell the story from the beginning to the end. (Summarizing)

• How do you think PAL Hershey feels about being a reading therapy dog? (Inferring)

II. Establish a Daily Read Aloud Time

Establish a daily read aloud time to help build language acquisition, communication, and literacy skills. If your child enjoyed this book, select other books related to therapy dogs, service dogs or animals. Selecting read aloud books that incorporate your child's interests allow them to strengthen comprehension skills by connecting the book to their own lives, connecting the book to other books on the same topic, and connecting reading to larger universal concepts.

(Additional books associated with topics such as therapy dogs, friendship, kindness, acceptance, patience, and perseverance align with goals from this book.)

Select read aloud books where children see themselves, and other children, people, animals, cultures, and communities to help children make stronger life connections and better understand themselves and their world.

Don't forget to reread <u>The ABC's of Hershey: The Reading Therapy Dog.</u> If your child enjoyed this book, rereading is a wonderful way to help children strengthen their reading, fluency, and accuracy. Rereading also helps children develop a larger vocabulary, while helping each child identify themselves as a "reader". In addition, rereading is very comforting and reassuring to children. Rereading helps children increase their vocabulary. When children read the same book multiple times, they become more familiar and comfortable with a larger number of new vocabulary words.

Rereading is a source of comfort for children (it additionally increases oral reading fluency). Rereading stories aloud helps children become aware of patterns of text. It also allows children to read a familiar text or story without stopping or pausing, making reading more enjoyable for them.

Each reread allows a child to look more closely at the pattern of the text, the illustrations, and the connection between the printed word and the corresponding illustration. It can support a child's reading comprehension development by allowing them to discuss, in more detail, the main idea or gist of the book or story.

Rereading also supports children's reading confidence. Rereading a familiar text allows a child to become more confident and self-assured in their reading abilities. Children, through rereading, can make stronger connections between themselves and the book, and between the book and other books that may share similar features (characters, main idea, themes).

III. Incorporate Literacy into Your Family Time

Make literacy development an ongoing, interactive element of your daily life. In addition to the routine of daily read aloud time, playing word games is a fun, engaging and beneficial way to strengthen literacy skills.

- **Tongue Twisters** help children improve their pronunciation skills. They also are great vocal exercises for children that can result in better voice clarity and articulation. After reading this book, use PAL Hershey to create fun, silly tongue twisters. Have this activity be a shared experience with your child and allow it to be as creative and silly as you would like. Creating tongue twisters also provides an additional opportunity to expand your child's vocabulary with new or unfamiliar words.

A couple of examples include:

"Happy, hungry Hershey headed home."
"Hershey hopes Henry hears husky horses."

- **Rhyming Words** used deliberately throughout this book, help children learn about patterns and structures of written and spoken language. Recognizing rhyme is a key component of literacy development. Rhyming words in stories or poems can help emphasize sentence patterns and help make reading more memorable for children.

Use the alphabet letters from PAL Hershey's book to extend new word patterns for children.

An example might include:

> Reread page 3 with the letter "C" and emphasize the word "face".
> Reread page 4 with the letter "D" and emphasize the word "place".

Have children identify the two rhyming words: "face" and "place". Brainstorm additional words that rhyme with the "ace" ending. Write them down and create silly sentences about PAL Hershey.

Repeat using rhyming words found throughout the book.

Create a poster or word wall of rhyming words from Hershey's ABC book. Add to the list of words as you discover new rhyming words from other books.

- **Reread the Story** and create new action words for PAL Hershey. For example:

> "S is for smiling" could become "S is for sitting".
> "T is for treasuring" could become "T is for thanking".

Create new action words or verbs for each of PAL Hershey's ABC pages. Illustrate them and have fun.

- **Expand Vocabulary** by selecting words from the book that are new or interesting to your child. Help your child become a "word collector" by discussing the meaning of those selected words, finding synonyms for them, and rereading the book using your child's new vocabulary words. For example:

> "Frolicking" can lead to a discussion about the root or main word, "frolic".

Using the illustration and surrounding words in the sentence, help your child use these context clues to describe the meaning of "frolic". Alternative suggestions for "frolic" can then be compared to definitions from a dictionary. Illustrations of "frolicking" can be added alongside the synonyms. Word collections can be recorded in notebooks, binders or personalized word detective books.

• **Word banks** are another fun and easy way to help children expand their vocabulary. Collecting words related to a specific subject or topic allows children to record interesting vocabulary words, create personalized illustrations of the new words and use their new vocabulary words in writing stories. New vocabulary words can then be categorized and sorted by a variety of categories, themes, and subjects.

• **Puns** are an excellent form of word play that makes use of multiple meanings of a term or similar sounding sounds to create a humorous effect. Specifically, this book uses "animal puns" to create additional humor.

For example:

"Pawsitively" fun ideas is deliberately used to infuse a dog pun. Discuss the pun with your child and help him determine the message the author was trying to convey. "Pawsitively" can be translated into "positive." Try writing your own animal puns with your child after reading several puns found in <u>The ABC's of Hershey: The Reading Therapy Dog.</u>

For additional "pawsome" fun, create a pun display of your child's ideas and puns. We imagine you and your child will create many "a-dog-able" puns and have a "paw-fect" time together.

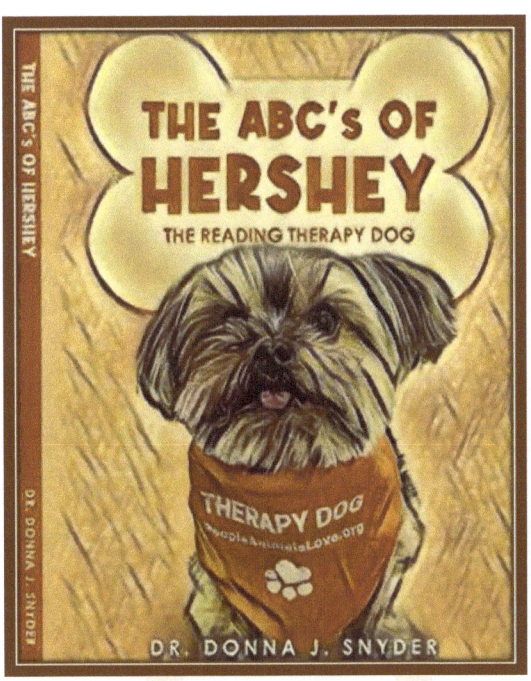

Goals and Objectives of
The ABC's of Hershey: The Reading Therapy Dog

This book was created to actively engage readers with the role of a reading therapy dog. Many questions commonly asked about reading therapy dogs are creatively answered in a child-friendly, developmentally appropriate format.

Through rhythm, rhyme, and an alphabetical sequence, this book is designed to provide students with a deeper understanding of the role of a reading therapy dog. It is created to follow the daily sequence that a reading therapy dog follows from early morning until the actual reading session occurs at the school, with children. PAL Hershey "paw-lights" requirements and best practices to follow when inviting a reading therapy dog into the classroom. He addresses topics such as:

- **Therapy Dog Assessments, Temperament Testing, and Registration**

Therapy dogs should always display a friendly, patient, calm and gentle manner. PAL Hershey highlights the desired temperament throughout the book. He models the desired behaviors of a therapy dog by being well-tempered, friendly, social, and happy to be around children. He is patient, gentle and enjoys being petted and touched by children as they read to him. He is attentive to each reader. PAL Hershey also highlights his Canine Good Citizen (CGC) awards and therapy dog certificates that he has earned through the AKC. He also purposefully displays his PAL bandana as the form of identification to indicate he is a registered therapy dog with People Animals Love (PAL), an AKC recognized therapy dog association. As a member of the registered therapy dog team, PAL Hershey's handler also wears a PAL t-shirt or sweatshirt to each school visit. PAL Hershey also emphasizes the importance of consistently following PAL therapy dog procedures and policies associated with PAL registration. Additionally, a copy of PAL Hershey's current vaccination records is always included in his backpack.

- **At Home Preparation, Before Arriving at School**

PAL Hershey highlights the importance of school readiness by having a balanced breakfast, exercising, grooming and personal hygiene care, and preparing his therapy backpack. Items included in his school backpack are displayed to engage the reader in discussing the types of items that help ensure a successful school-based session. It is important for a reading therapy dog to have access to a small bowl of water, if needed, during each session. In addition to his short leash, a mat, small rug or blanket are also included in his backpack. Having a small mat allows a therapy dog to go to a familiar location, if he/she becomes overly tired during the session. In addition, it provides a safe, secure space that the dog knows. Often, the reading therapy dog may want to sit or lie on the mat as the child reads the story to him/her. Additionally, anti-bacterial wipes are also included in PAL Hershey's backpack and are provided to each reader at the beginning of each session.

- **Expectations for Reading Therapy Dogs at School**

Therapy dog organizations maintain expectations, procedures, and policies for the therapy dogs serving in their organizations. While temperament testing, obedience skills, and health requirements are often included in formal therapy animal assessment and evaluation, individual organizations may also have unique and personalized requirements. PAL Hershey demonstrates the importance of reviewing PAL organizational requirements while also knowing the overall guidelines and policies associated with the school that he is visiting. When a reading therapy dog arrives at a school for the first visit, it is important to have an introductory session with the teacher and students to establish the purpose and expectations for having the reading therapy dog in the classroom. A read aloud, such as <u>The ABC's of Hershey: The Reading Therapy Dog</u> helps explain those expectations in a light-hearted and easy to understand format.

- **Best Practices for Reading Aloud to a Reading Therapy Dog**

PAL Hershey models desired behaviors to help ensure a successful and well-loved reading session. When a reading therapy dog is invited into a classroom to listen to children read, the individual readers need to have an opportunity to "meet and greet" their furry listener. Children should be pre-selected by the teacher, before the arrival of the reading therapy dog. A list of the selected children should be given to the handler as well as a schedule outlining the time blocks for each reader. If the session occurs outside of the classroom, it is important to have one staff member who is designated as the greeter to accompany each child to and from the therapy dog reading location. To provide a welcoming and nurturing environment, a quiet, cozy corner of a classroom, library or other similar location should be used. The environment should be arranged to limit potential distractions or interruptions. The positioning of the reader, therapy dog and handler are also important. PAL Hershey deliberately positions himself comfortably between the reader and his handler. Sitting between the two individuals allows PAL Hershey to see the book, listen patiently as the book is read, and enjoy some belly rubs, pats, or gentle touches from the reader, while staying close to the handler. The handler always has a hold of PAL Hershey's short leash, either in her hand, around her wrist or tucked gently under her legs.

During the session, PAL Hershey provides an interactive experience for the reader by carefully listening as the story is read. When the reader encounters a new or challenging vocabulary word or is unsure of the word or its meaning, the handler relies on the therapy dog to assume the role of the learner. The handler can assist the reader and help teach the meaning of the new word by posing questions that involve the reading therapy dog. Examples such as, "Wow, I don't think PAL Hershey has ever heard that word before. Let's see if the illustration can help PAL Hershey better understand the meaning of the word." Or, "PAL Hershey would love to know more about that new word. Do you think we could both explain it to him?" Pausing briefly to pose questions during the reading session can help each reader monitor their own reading comprehension and maintain interest in their reading. (Please see the resource section related to "Extend the Fun with PAL Hershey for Parents, Guardians, Volunteers and Para-Educators: Incorporate Questions Before, During and After Reading <u>The ABC's of Hershey: The Reading Therapy Dog</u> for sample questions.) As the session continues, ensure each reader receives supportive and encouraging comments. Comments that are specific, meaningful, and purposeful are most helpful to boost students' self-awareness, self-monitoring, and motivation for reading. Comments such as "PAL Hershey loved the expression that you used on this page. You read it with such excitement when you saw the exclamation point. It helped PAL Hershey better understand how excited the little girl was." Or, "PAL Hershey loved how you showed him the illustration of the speckled lizard as you used it to discover the new vocabulary word 'speckled' and then explained it to him."

As the session comes to a close, the handler should remind the reader when the final two minutes are approaching. A reminder allows the reader to complete a final page, summarize the session, mark the page where the session ended, and make a plan for continuing reading in the classroom or at home. Allow time for the reader to end the session by giving the dog a warm belly rub, pat or "paw-shake". PAL Hershey ends his sessions by providing each reader with a personalized bookmark. He also encourages each reader to continue daily reading at home. He thanks each reader and invites them to join him again in the near future. A general guideline is 60 minutes for a reading session, divided into four sessions of fifteen minutes for each reader. This guideline is important as the therapy dog has been attentive, remaining in a sit or down position for an extended period of time. A quick stretch break between readers allows the therapy dog to be attentive and ready for the next student to begin his reading period.

- **Importance of Emotional and Relationship Development**

PAL Hershey models patience, companionship, support, and positive social interactions. He provides a trusting environment where students can build and strengthen their self-confidence and self-esteem. Students reading to a therapy dog often believe they are also helping the dog, which often leads to a sense of accomplishment, greater concentration, and a stronger inner motivation for reading. Gentle and patient reading therapy dogs allow students to experience a relaxed and nonjudgmental atmosphere to practice their reading skills. Students often feel less pressure when reading to a therapy dog than reading aloud to a classroom of peers. The welcoming environment that a therapy dog creates results in a trusting environment for students and can help them gain more confidence, feel more connected and develop a greater sense of empathy. PAL Hershey's calm and gentle manner allows students to bond easily with him, helping the students to feel respected, accepted, and trusted. Students' positive experiences with reading therapy dogs can lead to more positive attitudes toward learning and encouraging prosocial behaviors in the classroom.

Benefits of Reading Therapy Dogs

The history of dogs partnering with humans as therapy dogs dates back to the 18th century. Research for the past several decades documents the effects of therapy dogs related to emotional, social, physical, and educational support for children.

Many schools and libraries are now incorporating therapy dogs into their instructional programs. Related to literacy development, reading therapy dogs provide many benefits to students. However, the use of animal assisted literacy programs should supplement, not replace, the reading instructional program provided by the classroom teacher. Reading therapy dogs can help to motivate, engage, and provide positive reading experiences for students.

Reading therapy dogs have been shown to benefit students' literacy development in the following ways:

- Provide a calming presence for students
- Reduce stress often encountered when learning to read or when learning to reading is difficult
- Improve self-confidence
- Decrease absenteeism
- Provide motivation to read and write
- Provide non-stressful, non-judgmental environments to practice reading

- Reduce self-consciousness of reading
- Provide opportunities for students to enjoy reading and writing
- Increase motivation when reading
- Improve reading rate, accuracy, and comprehension
- Improve reading fluency
- Provide a relaxed atmosphere to practice reading skills
- Build new relationships
- Promote emotional regulation among young readers
- Reduce anxiety in children by sharing a calm and friendly demeanor during reading sessions
- Encourage increased attention span and allow students to focus on the reading task at hand
- Improve memory retention through a more relaxed state of mind, allowing children the opportunity to absorb and better retain more information.

References for the benefits of reading therapy dogs are included in this resource section.

Glossary

Animal-Assisted Activities (AAA) - AAA provides opportunities for education, motivation, or recreation to enhance the quality of life for others. These activities can be delivered in a wide variety of settings by volunteers, paraprofessionals, or professionals in conjunction with qualified animals who meet specific guidelines and criteria.

Animal Assisted Education (AAE) – AAE is a planned and structured intervention directed or delivered by educational or related service professionals. The intervention has specific educational or academic goals. The AAE process is evaluated and documented.

Animal-Assisted Intervention (AAI) - AAI is an interdisciplinary term that is used to describe activities that intentionally incorporate animals into human services, education, healthcare, or similar fields. It is a larger term that includes Animal-Assisted Activities (AAA), Animal-Assisted Education (AAE), Animal-Assisted Therapy (AAT), Animal-Assisted Special Programs (AASP), and Animal-Assisted Placement Programs (AAPP).

Animal-Human Bond - Mutually beneficial and dynamic relationship between people and animals that positively influence the health and well being of both.

American Kennel Club (AKC) – Founded in 1884, the nonprofit AKC is the recognized and trusted expert in breed, health, and training information for all dogs. The AKC Family Dog Program includes the 4 levels of the Canine Good Citizen program: AKC S.T.A.R. Puppy, Canine Good Citizen, AKC Community Canine, and AKC Urban CGC. AKC Family Dog also includes AKC Therapy Dog, AKC Trick Dog, AKC FIT Dog, AKC Temperament Test and AKC Virtual Home Manners. A dog must be registered by one of the recognized AKC therapy dog organizations to earn AKC Therapy Dog titles.

Emotional Support Dog – This companion animal helps its owner cope with the challenges associated with emotional and mental health conditions by providing comfort with their presence. Emotional support dogs are not covered under the Americans with Disabilities Act but have special status under the Fair Housing Act.

Dog Handler – This person is trained, tested, and registered as part of a dog therapy team. This person functions as the therapy animal's advocate at all times.

People Animals Love (PAL) - A nonprofit organization that is recognized by the AKC as a therapy dog organization. PAL provides educational material to volunteers, screens both volunteers and pets, and provides liability insurance for when the animal and handler are volunteering in a therapy setting. PAL is based in the metropolitan DC area.

Reading Therapy Dog - A therapy dog that is trained to listen to children read books aloud, through a friendly, nonjudgmental, calm demeanor. They create a safe, comfortable and supportive environment.

Service Dog – A service dog is often referred to as an "assistance dog". A service dog is trained to perform tasks and to do work that eases their handler's disabilities. Service dogs help their handlers attain safety and independence. Most service dogs have a "no petting" policy. The most common service dogs include guide, hearing, medical alert, mobility, autism service, and psychiatric service dogs. Any business or facility that serves the public must allow service dogs to accompany people with disabilities in the areas of the facility where the public is permitted.

Therapy Dog – A dog trained to provide affection, comfort, and support to people in various settings. Therapy dogs are trained to interact with all kinds of people, not just their handlers or owners. Therapy dogs are trained in basic obedience skills. They are trained to be patient, kind, friendly and gentle with a wide variety of people in different settings. Some therapy dogs serve as reading therapy dogs. All therapy dogs must meet medical, temperament testing and other assessments and requirements associated with the therapy animal organization of which they are members. They also must be registered with a recognized therapy dog organization. Therapy dogs wear some type of identification, tag, vest, or accessory that indicates that they are a registered therapy dog. Often the American Kennel Club (AKC) Canine Good Citizen (CGC) skill test is used as one component of the assessment.

Therapy Dog Team - The handler and dog who have been trained to provide interactions such as visiting nursing homes, hospitals, libraries, senior centers, and schools.

Acknowledgements

PAL Hershey has earned several American Kennel Club (AKC) Therapy Dog awards and certificates. He is also an AKC Canine Good Citizen (CGC, CGCA, CGCU). PAL Hershey is registered with People Animals Love (PAL), a therapy animal organization serving the Washington, DC metropolitan area. For additional information on AKC recognized therapy dog organizations, please visit:

American Kennel Club at *www.akc.org* A list of AKC recognized therapy dog organizations can also be found on their website. A dog must be registered by one of these organizations to be eligible to earn and receive AKC Therapy Dog titles.

Many therapy animal organizations also require that animals earn the AKC Canine Good Citizen (CGC) certificate. The AKC CGC skill test is a certification program that evaluates dogs in simulated everyday situations in a relaxed environment. It is often used to demonstrate that a dog displays good manners and responsible dog ownership for their owners. The CGC tests are divided into four levels:

AKC S.T.A.R. Puppy
Canine Good Citizen (CGC)
Canine Good Citizen Advanced (CGCA)
Canine Good Citizen Urban (CGCU)

AKC Therapy Dog program recognizes the therapy work performed by dogs through their accepted organizations. AKC Therapy Dog titles are earned based on the number of visits a dog and handler complete. AKC Therapy Dog titles are earned in six levels:

AKC Therapy Dog Novice (THDN)
AKC Therapy Dog (THD)
AKC Therapy Dog Advanced (THDA)
AKC Therapy Dog Excellent (THDX)
AKC Therapy Dog Distinguished (THDD)
AKC Therapy Dog Supreme (THDS)

For information related to the AKC registered therapy animal organization that PAL Hershey is registered with, please visit:

People Animals Love (PAL) at *www.peopleanimalslove.org* PAL is an AKC recognized therapy dog association. The PAL mission is to "use the human-animal bond to comfort the lonely, ease the pain of the sick and enrich people's lives". PAL therapy animal teams visit schools, libraries, hospitals, jails, hospice facilities, universities, long-term care facilities and other sites unique to the DC metropolitan area.

Meet the Team

PAL Hershey: PAL Hershey is a confident, curious, and lovable five-pound Yorkie. He is also, proudly, a registered therapy dog with People Animals Love (PAL). PAL Hershey has a zest for life and LOVES his volunteer work at many locations throughout the Washington, DC metropolitan area. PAL Hershey spreads joy and happiness during his visits to nursing homes, assisted living centers, senior centers, homeless shelters, centers for adults with disabilities, federal government agencies, libraries, and schools. He also volunteers his services virtually through ZOOM sessions for both children and senior citizens. PAL Hershey greatly admires young readers and supports their academic, social, and emotional development. PAL Hershey has completed many training sessions and has also earned the following American Kennel Club (AKC) awards and titles:

- AKC Canine Good Citizen (CGC)
- AKC Advanced Canine Good Citizen (CGGA)
- AKC Urban Canine Good Citizen (CGCU)
- AKC Therapy Dog Novice (THDN)
- AKC Therapy Dog (THD)
- AKC Therapy Dog Advanced (THDA)
- AKC Therapy Dog Excellent (THDX)
- AKC Novice Trick Dog

PAL Hershey has also successfully completed additional assessments and required testing through People Animals Love (PAL) to become a registered therapy dog for PAL.

Dr. Donna Snyder: Donna is the author of the book and the handler of PAL Hershey. Donna has served her professional career in the field of education. She is a former elementary school teacher, district-level curriculum specialist, principal, principal mentor, Director of Early Childhood and Elementary Education for a diverse, urban school system, and an adjunct university professor. Donna has been responsible for leading school improvement initiatives for K-12 urban schools. She is an experienced and successful school turnaround principal, focused on increasing academic achievement of students in underperforming schools. Donna is also a consultant to educational organizations related to school improvement and instructional delivery. She has vast experience in both public and private education. Donna has served as the Executive Director for an educational nonprofit organization, and the Chief Education Officer for a diverse K-16 international educational company, serving over 45,000 students annually. She often presents at national and international conferences related to instruction, assessment, school climate, school leadership and school improvement.

Donna has been a dog lover, owner and advocate her entire life. She and PAL Hershey volunteer multiple times weekly throughout the Washington, DC metropolitan area. Donna is also an active member of the nonprofit organization People Animals Love (PAL) and serves in various roles to support the organization's mission. Donna is proud to serve on the Board of Directors of PAL.

Stay Connected with PAL Hershey

I LOVE listening to stories! I also love receiving your letters and messages. I hope that you will share your favorite books and stories with me! I am always excited to learn about books that you LOVE! Just like you, I want to continue to grow and learn. I also love to see your pictures and illustrations about your favorite books, authors, and stories.

You can write to me at: HersheyAKCtherapydog@gmail.com and I will respond to your letters and messages. You may also want to follow me on Instagram at: @hersheykiss_yorkie

I hope to hear from you soon!

Additional Sources

Anderson, K. L., & Olson, M. R. (2006). The value of a dog in a classroom of children with severe emotional disorders. Anthrozoös, 19(1), 35-49.

Barker, S.B., & Wolen, A.R. (2008). The benefits of human-companion animal interaction: A review. Journal of Veterinary Medical Education, 35(4), 487-495.

Barrett, L. Paws to read @ your library. Virginia Libraries. Retrieved June 17, 2021, from https://virginialibrariesjournal.org/articles/10.21061/valib.v49i3.909/

Brelsford, V. L., Meints, K., Gee, N. R., & Pfeffer, K. (2017). Animal-assisted interventions in the classroom – A systematic review. International Journal of Environmental Research and Public Health, 14(7), Article 669. https://doi:10.3390/ijerph14070669

Gee, N. R., Church, M.T., & Altobelli, C.L. (2010). Preschoolers make fewer errors on an object categorization task in the presence of a dog. Anthrozoos, 23(3), 223-230.

Grove, Christine et al. "Therapy Dogs in Educational Settings: Guidelines and Recommendations for Implementation." Frontiers in veterinary science vol. 8 655104. 8 Jun. 2021, doi: 10.3389/fvets.2021.655104

Hediger, K., & Turner, D. C. (2014). Can dogs increase children's attention and concentration performance? A randomised controlled trial. Human-Animal Interaction Bulletin, 2(2), 21- 39.

https://www.4pawscenter.org/images/pdf/readers-Canine_Buddies.pdf
https://dogsconnect.net.au/reading-dogs-in-schools-boosting-learning-and-we ll-being.

Intermountain Therapy Animals. 2011. Available: http://www.therapyanimals.org/R.E.A.D.html. Accessed 10 December 2014.

Jalongo MR. "What are all these dogs doing at school?" Using therapy dogs to promote children's reading practice. Child Educ. 2005;81(3): 152–158

Kirnan, J., Siminerio, S., & Wong, Z. (2015). The impact of a therapy dog program on children's reading skills and attitudes toward reading. Early Childhood Education Journal, 44, 637- 651. https://doi.org/10.1007/s10643-015-0747-9

Klotz K. Promoting humane education through Intermountain Therapy Animals' R.E.A.D. program. In Jalongo MR, editor. Teaching compassion: Humane education in early childhood. New York: Springer; 2014. pp. 175–195.

Ko, M. "Reading to Therapy Dogs Improves Literacy Attitudes in Second-Grade Students: Tufts Now. May 31, 2017. http://now.tufts.edu/news-releases/reading-therapy-dogs-improves-literacy=attitudes-second-grade-students-0.

Kropp, J. J., & Shupp, M. M. (2017). Review of the research: Are therapy dogs in classrooms beneficial? Forum on Public Policy Online, 2017(2). https://forumonpublicpolicy.com/wpcontent/uploads/2018/02/Final-Draft-Kropp-and-Shupp.pdf

Lane HB, Zavada DW. When reading gets ruff: canine-assisted reading programmes. Read Teach. 2013;67: 87–95.

Martin, S. (2001). READ is a pawsitive program for kids of all ages. Interactions, 19(3), 7-8.

Pillow-Price K, Yonts N, Stinson L. Sit, stay, read: Improving literacy skills using dogs! Dimensions of Early Childhood. 2014;42: 5–9. Available: http://www.southernearlychildhood.org/upload/pdf/SitStayRead_D42_1.pdf. Accessed 25 March 2015.

Shannon, M. A. R. Y. (2007). The benefits of children reading to dogs in public libraries and after school centers: An exploratory study. Unpublished master's thesis). City University of New York, Queens College, Flushing, NY. Retrieved from http://readtothedogs. org/READthesis. pdf. (2022). Retrieved 20 April 2022, from https://files.eric.ed.gov/fulltext/EJ1173578.pdf

Trammell, J.P. (2017). The effect of therapy dogs on exam stress and memory. Anthrozoos,30(4), 607-621.

Ward-Griffin, E., Klaiber, P., Collins, H.K., Owens, R.L., Coren, S., & Chen, F.S. (2018). Petting away pre-exam stress. The effect of therapy dog sessions on student well-being. Stress and Health.

Wheeler, L (2022). 4 Legged SEL: How to Start a Therapy Dog Program. Edutopia. Available: https://www.edutopia.org

6 Ways Therapy Dogs in Schools Help Students Succeed. Available: https://puppington.co

Thank You from PAL Hershey

**Thank you for being a "furever" friend.
You can cut out my picture and I will always stay close by when you read, draw, or share many new "paw-some" ideas!**

www.ingramcontent.com/pod-product-compliance
Lightning Source LLC
LaVergne TN
LVHW070435080526
838201LV00133B/281